Amazing Mysteries
MESSAGES FROM BEYOND

Anne Rooney

A⁺
Smart Apple Media

Smart Apple Media
P.O. Box 3263
Mankato, MN 56002

Printed in the United States of America

Library of Congress Cataloging-in-Publication Data

Rooney, Anne.
  Messages from beyond / by Anne Rooney.
      p. cm. -- (Amazing mysteries)
  Includes index.
  ISBN 978-1-59920-363-8 (hardcover)
  1. Parapsychology--Juvenile literature. I. Title.
  BF1031.R675 2010
  133.9--dc22
                          2009003398

Created by Q2AMedia
Editor: Honor Head
Art Director: Rahul Dhiman
Designer: Harleen Mehta
Picture Researchers: Dimple Bhorwal, Shreya Sharma
Line Artist: Sibi N. Devasia
Coloring Artists: Mahender Kumar, Subash Vohra

All words in **bold** can be found in the Glossary on pages 30–31.

Web site information is correct at time of going to press. However, the publishers cannot
accept liability for any information or links found on third-party web sites.

9 8 7 6 5 4 3 2 1

Contents

Life after Death?

Do the dead just lie in their graves, or do they live on in a **spirit world**? Some people believe they live on, and some say that they have heard messages from spirits.

Talking Spirits

Many people claim they have seen or talked with the spirits of dead people. These spirits may be helpful—they may warn of danger or show where to find things that have been lost—or they may want our help. There are tales of murdered spirits helping to find their own killers.

Face to Face

In 1971, Maria Gomez Pereira saw a strange mark on the kitchen floor of her house in Spain. She tried to clean it off, but it grew and appeared to look like a human face. Her husband smashed up the floor but more faces appeared. The town council dug up the floor and found buried skeletons. Many had their heads missing.

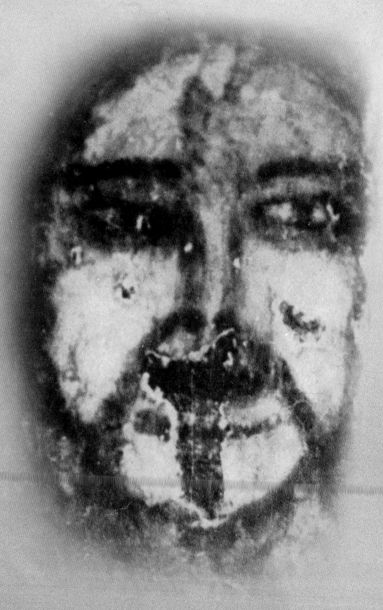

! This scary face appeared on the floor of a Spanish house.

4

Seeing the Future

Not all messages come from the dead or the past. Some people claim they can see into the future. They give strange and mysterious examples of having known something before it happened. Sometimes a dream reveals the truth, or an odd feeling turns out to be a warning.

SPOOKY!

In 1948, a **psychic** named Wolf Messing went to the city of Ashgabat, Turkmenistan to put on a show. As he walked the city streets, he felt that something terrible was going to happen. He cancelled his performances and left. Three days later the city was completely destroyed by a huge earthquake and 50,000 people were killed.

! This statue commemorates the earthquake that destroyed the city of Ashgabat, Turkmenistan, in 1948. Wolf Messing fled days before the disaster, after feeling a mysterious sense of dread.

It's Murder!

Murderers don't always get away with their terrible crimes—but it isn't usually the victim that gets them arrested!

A Bad Match

When Maria Marten fell in love with William Corder, her family knew her boyfriend had been in trouble with the law, but they couldn't stop Maria from seeing him. In 1827, Maria met William at the red barn near her house. The couple decided to run away and get married. Maria's family never saw her again.

! The red barn where Maria was murdered.

Murder at the Red Barn

William sent letters to Maria's family saying he and Maria were married. But Maria's stepmother had dreams telling her that Maria had been murdered. Her husband searched the red barn and found Maria's **decaying** body hidden in a sack. William's green handkerchief was tied around her neck.

Plays and Stories

Based on this **evidence**, the police tracked William down in London in 1828 and charged him with the murder of Maria. He was found guilty and hanged. Thousands of people watched the **execution**. The story caught the public's imagination. People were intrigued that the stepmother's dream lead her to find the body. Songs and plays about the murder in the red barn were very popular.

SPOOKY!

Psychic Robert Cracknell was nearly arrested for a murder he tried to solve. In 2005 an Australian girl was murdered in her car in London. Cracknell told a journalist about an object on the back seat of the car. When the journalist asked the police about the object, they said that only the murderer would have known about it. The police wanted to arrest Cracknell, but he told them that the murderer was a man with a scarred face who was in prison for another crime. This turned out to be true!

! The murder of Maria Marten made a scary but exciting story!

Evil Husband

Mothers often have a keen sense of knowing their children are in danger. Elva Zona Heaster's mother felt that way about her daughter and new husband, Erasmus Trout Shue. On January 23, 1897, Elva was found dead at her house. Erasmus seemed upset, but he wouldn't let the doctor examine the body properly. In the coffin, Elva's neck was wedged between a rolled-up sheet and a pillow.

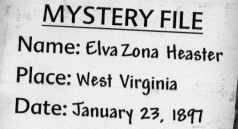

MYSTERY FILE

Name: Elva Zona Heaster

Place: West Virginia

Date: January 23, 1897

A Bloody Sheet

Before Elva was buried, her mother took the sheet from the coffin with her. It had a strange smell. She decided to wash it, and the water immediately turned bright red, like blood. Elva's mother jumped back in horror. When she looked again, the sheet was stained pink, and she couldn't wash the stain out.

! Elva was already in her grave when she apparently told her mother about her murder.

A Visit from the Grave

For four nights, the ghost of Elva appeared to her mother and told a terrible tale. Erasmus had beaten her, and one day he had strangled her. Elva's mother told the local **prosecutor**. Elva's body was dug up and examined—her neck was broken. She had been strangled to death.

Convicted by a Ghost

Erasmus was arrested and tried for Elva's murder. In court, Elva's mother repeated the ghost's words, and Erasmus was found guilty and put in prison. It is the only case of a ghost's evidence being listened to in an American court.

SPOOKY!

Medium Doris Stokes claimed to have helped the police solve two murders in the United States. She said that the spirit of murdered Vic Weiss told her details about his killer. Weiss's body was found tied up and shot in his Rolls Royce in Hollywood in 1979. The murder has still not been solved.

! Doris Stokes claimed she helped the police solve murders—by talking with the victims.

Past Lives

Some people say they have lived and died before, and have been **reincarnated** to live again. They say they can remember what they did in a past life!

Stepping Back in Time

In the 1970s, a Welsh housewife using the false name Jane Evans seemed to be able to "remember" six previous lives. Her earlier lives ranged from York, England, at the time of the ancient Romans, to a life as a nun in Iowa, in the 20th century.

Killed by the Mob

In one of her earlier lives, Jane claims she was a Jewish woman named Rebecca living in York, England. She said there was a **massacre** of Jews in 1189, and she and her two children hid in the cellar of a church just outside York. She was killed there by a Christian mob.

! Jews were often attacked by Christians in medieval Europe, as Jane Evans claims she was in an earlier life.

! Many people claim they can remember past lives when they are hypnotized.

Hidden Cellar

A historian located a church outside York, England where he thought "Rebecca" died, but it did not have a cellar. When the church was **excavated** six months later, though, workmen found a hidden cellar. It was just as Evans had described it, and no one else had known about it.

SPOOKY!

Sometimes, people are **hypnotized** so they can remember earlier lives. The hypnotist asks questions and helps them to "unlock" their memories. The previous lives described by Jane Evans were recalled under hypnosis. Were these real past lives that she remembered? Perhaps people just remember historical information they have read.

Going Home

In 1948, Swarnlata Mishra was three years old and traveling with her father when they passed the town of Katni, India. They were 100 miles (160 km) from their home, but Swarnlata claimed she had lived here in her last life. Over the next few years she told her father details of her former life. She had been called Biya Pathak, and had a husband and two sons. She described her house and life in great detail. Biya had died in 1939.

All Present and Correct

When Swarnlata was ten, a researcher found the house she had described. Some of the members of her old family were still alive and Swarnlata went to meet them. She recognized all of them, and knew many private details about their lives. She remembered everything as it had been in 1939, when Biya died.

SPOOKY!

At three years old, the famous Indian sitar player Ravi Shankar surprised his parents by asking for toys from the house where he lived before. When he was six years old, Ravi told his parents a dreadful story—he said he had been killed by two relatives who cut his head off with a razor. A boy of six had been killed in this way six months before Ravi was born. Ravi has a birthmark like a razor cut around his neck, too.

! Ravi Shankar claims he remembers past lives—even one when he was murdered!

Reincarnation

Buddhism teaches that every soul is reincarnated—reborn in a different body—many times. The soul may come back as another person, or as an animal. At each stage, the soul works toward becoming perfect. Finally, it escapes the cycle of reincarnation and becomes a **buddha**.

! The current Dalai Lama expects to be reincarnated when he dies.

The Dalai Lama

The Dalai Lama is a Buddhist leader. When the Dalai Lama dies, Buddhists believe his soul goes into the body of the new Dalai Lama. They believe the new Dalai Lama can recognize objects belonging to the last Dalai Lama. They test small children, who are born soon after the Dalai Lama's death, to find one who can recognize something belonging to the old leader. This child then becomes the new Dalai Lama.

Ship of Death

Most passengers were very excited about traveling on the new **liner**, the *RMS Titanic*. It was the largest and most luxurious ship ever built and set sail from Southampton, England, to New York, on its first voyage in 1912.

A Terrible Accident

At midnight on April 14, 1912, the *Titanic* hit an iceberg and sank, killing more than 1,500 people. The owners of the ship thought it was unsinkable, so it did not have enough lifeboats.

! People escaped in lifeboats or jumped into the freezing sea as the *Titanic* sank.

SPOOKY!

In 1898—14 years before the sinking of the *Titanic*—Morgan Robertson wrote a novel about a luxury liner called the *Titan*. It was thought to be unsinkable, and had too few lifeboats. At midnight one night in April, the *Titan* strikes an iceberg and sinks, killing nearly everyone on board—just like the *Titanic*!

The wreck of the *Titanic* still lies at the bottom of the ocean.

Uneasy Feeling

Not everyone believed the claims that the ship was unsinkable. Several people had an uneasy feeling about the liner and cancelled their trips, including two famous bankers and the owner of the Hershey chocolate bar company, Milton Hershey. Also, 22 men who worked stoking the engines of the ship did not turn up to work on time and the *Titanic* sailed without them, saving their lives.

Strange Warning

As the *Titanic* sailed past the Isle of Wight, a woman who had gone to watch started screaming, "It's going to sink! That ship is going to sink! Do something! Are you so blind that you are going to let them drown? Save them! Save them!" No one took any notice of her warning.

GRAVE TALES

Young Donald Wollam, born in Illinois in 1960, was terrified of water, but fascinated by the Titanic. *He found out all he could about it, but also seemed to know details not in his own books. He spoke of a girl and boy playing on the ship. Donald drowned at age 18. Later, his mother heard an elderly woman who had been a passenger on the* Titanic *say she used to play on the ship with her brother. Had Donald been on the* Titanic *in a previous life?*

Dreams Talk

Many people believe they receive messages in dreams. Usually the messages are hard to understand, but sometimes a dream message can be perfectly clear— and seem to tell the future.

! Did President Abraham Lincoln foresee his own death in a dream?

Warning the President

American President Abraham Lincoln told his wife, a member of his government, and his bodyguard about a strange dream he had. In it, he heard crying in the White House. When he went to investigate, he found his own body laid out ready for burial. In the dream, he was told that the president had been **assassinated**. Lincoln had the dream for three nights in a row.

Date with Destiny

On April 14, 1865, about two weeks after he'd had the dream, Lincoln set out for the Ford Theater with his wife. His bodyguard advised him not to go, but Lincoln had promised to take his wife to the show. As he watched the performance, a man named John Wilkes Booth walked into President Lincoln's box and shot him dead.

Find the Sphinx!

The earliest known dream **premonition** was nearly 3,500 years ago. The Egyptian pharaoh Thutmose IV had a dream in which a god came to him and told him to clear away the sand in a particular area. Here he would find the Sphinx that had been lost under the sands of Egypt for hundreds of years. The pharaoh ordered the sand to be cleared, and the Sphinx was uncovered.

SPOOKY!

Nine-year-old Florence Conners was with her mother in a train in Kansas City, Missouri. She began staring at a woman passenger. When the woman got off, Florence ran across the train to watch her. Her mother told her to sit down, but Florence said, "I want to see how she dies!" The woman stepped in front of a horse-drawn wagon pulling a heavy load of metal and was killed instantly.

The Sphinx lay buried under sand for centuries until a dream revealed exactly where it was.

Terrible Tragedy

In 1966, a terrible disaster happened in the Welsh village of Aberfan. A huge mountain of coal waste slipped and collapsed on to the village school, killing 116 children. A large number of people reported having dreamed about the disaster in advance.

Pointy Hat

One victim was a woman from Plymouth who said she saw an old school in a valley, a coal miner, and coal pouring down a mountain. She saw a little boy at the bottom of the mountain, and then rescue workers, one with a strange pointed hat. She told friends and neighbors about the dream. The disaster happened later that week. She saw the same little boy and the rescue worker with the pointy hat on the television news.

SPOOKY!

So many people reported having dreams **predicting** the Aberfan disaster that the British government set up the British Premonitions Bureau. They thought that if people could report premonitions then perhaps some disasters might be avoided. A similar office was set up in New York. Both eventually closed because no useful premonitions were reported.

A mountain of coal waste buried victims at Aberfan. Many people said they had seen it in their dreams.

Danger on the Battlefield

Soldiers know they risk death in battle, so it's not surprising that many have premonitions of death and are then killed. Some have very precise dreams of what will happen, and have even warned other people.

A Week to Live

Before the battle of Fair Oaks in the Civil War, a volunteer soldier told his friends that he dreamed he only had a week to live. He described a battle which would take place in seven days. He said which men would die and how and where they would be found. It all happened a week later, including his death, just as he had said.

! There were many reports of people foretelling their death or deaths of others in the Civil War.

GRAVE TALES

In 1979, David Booth phoned American Airlines with a strange warning. He had dreamed that an American Airlines plane, a DC-10, had crashed in flames among tall buildings. A few days later, an American Airlines DC-10 took off from O'Hare Airport, Chicago. An engine fell off the plane, and it then crashed into buildings, killing everyone on board.

19

Talking Spirits

Dead bodies cannot speak—but what about dead spirits? Electronic Voice Phenomena—or EVP—are electronic recordings of sounds that some people say are made by the spirits of dead people.

Birds and Spirits

In 1959, retired Swedish opera singer, Friedrich Jurgensen, used a tape recorder to record bird songs. When he played the tape back, he found extra sounds that he had not heard at the time. They were voices. The first message he heard was, "Friedel, can you hear me? It's mommy. . ." Friedel was what his dead mother had called him!

Grave Answers

It seemed Friedrich was receiving messages from beyond the grave. He was able to pick out messages from other dead members of his family. He said he found a way to ask questions of the spirits and then find answers on the tapes. He claimed he even contacted figures from history, such as the famous painter, Vincent Van Gogh.

! Friedrich Jurgensen was using a tape recorder like this one to record bird songs. He claims he also recorded messages from the dead!

Recording Dead Voices

William O'Neil said he had help from a dead NASA scientist, Dr. George Jeffries Mueller, to make a machine that records spirit voices. By 1980, it was working well, and O'Neil had recorded more than 20 hours of talks with Mueller. Elsewhere, a woman named Sarah Estep says she made recordings of dead spirits including Beethoven and an 18th-century **lamplighter**.

Keeping Up with the Times

Spirit voices don't appear on just recordings. Many people claim to have spoken with the dead on the telephone and to have seen images of dead people appear on their televisions. One man even received messages in old-fashioned English on his computer from someone who said he had lived in the house 400 years before.

! Did a lamplighter talk to Sarah Estep from beyond the grave?

SPOOKY!

In the early 1950s, two Catholic priests in Milan, Italy, were recording religious chants, but a wire in their equipment kept breaking. One looked upward and asked his dead father for help. They were amazed to find a recorded message on their equipment from the priest's father. In a second message, the voice even used the father's nickname for his son.

! Could your television send you pictures of people from beyond the grave?

Heart to Heart

Organ transplants are life-saving operations. A working organ is taken from someone who has just died and is put into a patient whose own organ does not work properly. But is the organ all they get from the dead person?

MYSTERY FILE

Name: Claire Sylvia

Place: United States

Date: 1988

A New Woman

Claire Sylvia had a heart and lung transplant that saved her life. Once she had recovered from the operation, though, she was not quite the same person. She began to like beer, green peppers, and takeout chicken, which she had not liked before. Her daughter said she started to walk like a man. Claire found she was more forceful and confident.

! Claire Sylvia became a new woman after her heart and lung transplant.

Just Like Tim

Claire had a dream in which she met a young man called Tim L. and seemed to breathe him into her body. She decided to investigate. Eventually, she tracked down her organ **donor**—he had been a young man called Tim Lamirande who had died in a motorcycle accident. His family told her he liked beer, green peppers, and takeout chicken. Claire believes some of Tim's character was somehow held in his heart and had now passed into her.

! Many transplant organs come from accident victims.

GRAVE TALES

An eight-year-old girl received the heart of another girl who had been murdered. After the operation, she had terrible dreams about death. Her mother took her to a doctor. The details of her dreams were so clear that the doctor told the police about them. Using information from the girl's dreams, the police tracked down the man who had murdered the girl whose heart she had received. The dreams gave them the time and place of the murder and the weapon used.

Like Me, Like You

In October 2005, Lynda Gammons gave one of her kidneys to her husband Ian, who needed a transplant. Soon after the operation, Ian started to enjoy baking and gardening, although he had hated housework before. He even got a dog, when he previously liked only cats—but his wife liked dogs. The couple think some of Lynda's personality was carried into Ian through her kidney.

! Did Lynda Gammons give her personality to her husband, along with her kidney?

Art from a Heart

William Sheridan drew simple stick figures before his heart transplant operation in 2003. But after he had his new heart, he created amazing works of art. William tracked down the family of the man whose heart he had been given. He found his donor was a 24-year-old named Keith Neville, who had died in a car crash. Keith's mother said that her son loved art and was very artistic.

! An organ transplant gives someone life—but maybe the dead organ donor gets a new life as well.

GRAVE TALES

When Cheryl Cottle's husband, Terry, shot himself in the head, she donated his heart for a transplant. The man who received the heart, Sonny, later met up with Cheryl. The two fell in love and married soon after. Strangely, Sonny later also committed suicide by shooting himself in the throat.

Hard-Working Dead

Most people think that, however hard they have to work in their lifetime, at least they can have a rest when they're dead. But sometimes the dead seem to want to carry on working.

Speaking with the Dead

At a **séance**, a group of people get together with a medium to talk with the spirits. Many famous people, including President Abraham Lincoln and his wife, and Arthur Conan Doyle, who wrote the Sherlock Holmes stories, have used mediums to try to speak to the spirits of dead people.

! People at a séance touch hands and close their eyes to help them to connect with a spirit.

A Voice from the Past

Pearl Lenore Curran said she received messages from the spirit of Patience Worth, a **Quaker** girl born in England in the 1600s. The messages started to come through in 1913 when Pearl began to play with a **Ouija board**. Later, Pearl said she just heard the messages in her head. She wrote them down with a pen or typewriter, or **dictated** them to someone else.

A New Career

Patience told stories and poems that Pearl wrote down and later published. She even wrote several novels. Patience's writing gave many details of life in England long ago, and used words that Pearl would not have known. Patience became a famous and successful writer, even though she didn't start her new job until nearly 300 years after her death!

! Pearl Curran wrote books dictated to her by the spirit of a girl who had been dead for 300 years.

MYSTERY FILE

Name: Pearl Lenore Curran

Place: United States

Date: 1913

Music from Beyond the Grave

Beethoven was one of the world's greatest music **composers**. When he died in 1827, he left some of his works unfinished. Some say he was able to come back as a spirit more than 200 years later and ask Rosemary Brown to help him finish them.

Working with the Dead

Rosemary claims that she first saw the spirit of a great composer when she was a child. That time it was Franz Liszt, who died in 1886—though she didn't recognize him until years later.

SPOOKY!

The Irish poet W. B. Yeats worked with his wife, Georgie, a medium, to write his book, *A Vision*. The couple claimed to have contacted spirits of the dead who wanted to help Yeats write poetry.

Beethoven at work during his lifetime—has he continued to make music after his death?

Rosemary Brown
(right) claims to have
worked with several
dead composers.

Playing with Dead Hands

Rosemary wrote many musical
compositions that she said came from
dead composers. She said that she
would sit at the piano and the hands
of a dead composer would show her
how to play a piece of music. For some
composers, she would play a few bars,
then write down the notes. Others
would tell her what to write, but didn't
like her playing the piano because
she wasn't very good. Many musical
experts thought the compositions
were good enough to be by the
dead composer.

Shopping Liszt

The composers did not all stay
at the piano, or even in the
house. Rosemary reported that
Chopin liked modern clothes
and loved to watch television.
She said Liszt enjoyed going to
the supermarket with her but
was moody and could sulk for
weeks! Schubert was funny but
Rachmaninov was serious and
would never stay still.

Glossary

assassinated	killed for political reasons
buddha	a person who has been through several reincarnations and has gained enlightenment
Buddhism	a set of beliefs which began in India
composer	someone who writes music
decaying	rotting
dictate	to speak aloud for someone else to write down
donor	someone who gives something to another
evidence	proof, or a statement or object that might help to prove something
excavated	dug up
execution	a killing as a punishment in law
hypnotized	put into a trance-like state
lamplighter	a person who lit the street oil lamps every evening
liner	a large passenger ship for long journeys
massacre	a murder of many people
medium	someone who believes he or she can communicate with the spirits of dead people
organ transplant	an operation that puts an organ from a donor (often a dead person) into a patient whose own body does not work properly, replacing a damaged organ
Ouija board	a special board for communicating with spirits
predict	to say in advance what is going to happen

premonition	a feeling or vision that reveals something that will happen in the future
prosecutor	someone who accuses criminals in court
psychic	someone who has strange powers that enable him or her to read other people's minds, talk with the dead, or predict the future
Quaker	a member of the Quaker movement in the Christian religion. Quakers believe the voice of God speaks to them directly and guides them from within rather than through an organized church
reincarnated	brought back to life in a different body
séance	a meeting where people hold hands and call on the spirits of dead people
spirit world	the realm occupied by the spirits of dead people

Index

Webfinder

http://prairieghosts.com/mosthaunted.html
Describes the most haunted places in America

http://realghostsightings.net/
Ghost sightings—caught on tape!

http://paranormal.about.com/library/bltales_messages.htm
Ordinary people's tales of messages from beyond the grave